Shepherding
IN THE
Shadow of Death

Shepherding
IN THE
Shadow of Death

PAUL W. POWELL & MARK DANCE

LifeWay Press®
Nashville, Tennessee

Published by LifeWay Press®
© 2016 Mark Dance and Paul W. Powell
Reprinted December 2017

ISBN 978-1-4627-4180-9 • Item 005793274

To order additional copies of this resource, write to LifeWay
Resources Customer Service; One LifeWay Plaza; Nashville,
TN 37234; fax 615-251-5933; call toll free 800-458-2772;
order online at LifeWay.com; email orderentry@lifeway.com;
or visit the LifeWay Christian Store serving you.

Printed in the United States of America

Groups Ministry Publishing • LifeWay Resources
One LifeWay Plaza • Nashville, TN 37234

3 4 5 6 7 8 • 20 19 18

Contents

About the Authors

AFTER SEVENTEEN YEARS of successful ministry at Green Acres Baptist Church in Tyler, Texas, Paul W. Powell served as the president and CEO of the Annuity Board of the Southern Baptist Convention. Powell also served as dean of Baylor's George W. Truett Theological Seminary in 2001, where a 550-seat chapel is named in his honor. He earned degrees from Baylor University and Southwestern Baptist Theological Seminary, as well as five honorary doctorates.

Mark Dance serves as director of LifeWay Pastors. Prior to working with LifeWay, Dance pastored churches for twenty-seven years. He holds degrees from Howard Payne University (BBA), Southwestern Baptist Theological Seminary (MDiv), and Southern Baptist Theological Seminary (DMin).

@markdance; markdance.net; LifeWayPastors.com

Introduction

BUSY PASTORS ARE often called upon to function like a Leatherman Multi-Tool. One of your many sacred tasks is to shepherd people through the valley of the shadow of death. Funeral messages are usually needed on short notice, and are in addition to the many other preaching and ministry responsibilities you have.

This collection of funeral sermons will help busy pastors like you make the most out of your ministry to the bereaved. Since funerals provide a rare opportunity to speak a word of truth, hope, and comfort to the most spiritually diverse group we will ever face, we want you to be ready.

It is a privilege to cowrite this book with Paul Powell, my childhood pastor from Green Acres Baptist Church in Tyler, Texas. For over six decades, Dr. Powell has preached at least one funeral a month (approximately eight hundred total), which is probably not far off the pace for many pastors. The first twelve sermons are from him, as well as some helpful coaching in the appendices.

At Paul's request, I contributed the last three sermons and my name to this publication. My own ministry to pastors at LifeWay is an extension of Paul's ministry and legacy.

Mark Dance
Nashville, Tennessee

Chapter 1

It Is Well with My Soul

✳ Romans 8:35–39 ✳

IN 1871 CHICAGO was largely destroyed by fire. Horatio G. Spafford, a prominent Chicago businessman, lost most of what he owned in that fire. Shortly after this tragedy, Mr. Spafford put his wife and four daughters on a ship for passage to England. On a stormy November 22 night, the ship on which they were sailing was struck by a ship from Scotland, and in the confusion and turbulence that followed, his four daughters were swept overboard and lost. Upon arrival in England, Mrs. Spafford cabled her husband, beginning with these two words: "Saved alone."

On the first available ship, Mr. Spafford sailed to join his wife in England. While at sea, he asked the captain to alert him when they reached the spot where the ship had sunk. A steward later came to his cabin and said, "Mr. Spafford, we are almost at the spot." Mr. Spafford quickly went up to the deck, and as they passed over the watery grave of his daughters, the words of this song came to him:

When peace like a river,
attendeth my way,
When sorrows like sea billows roll;
Whatever my lot,
Thou hast taught me to say,
It is well, it is well with my soul.

In times like this we realize, maybe as never before, the need to be sure it is well with our soul. For that assurance we turn to the Word of God.

The apostle Paul writes,

> Who can separate us from the love of Christ? Can affliction or anguish or persecution or famine or nakedness or danger or sword? As it is written: Because of You we are being put to death all day long; we are counted as sheep to be slaughtered. No, in all these things we are more than victorious through Him who loved us. For I am persuaded that not even death or life, angels or rulers, things present or things to come, hostile powers, height or depth, or any other created thing will have the power to separate us from the love of God that is in Christ Jesus our Lord! (Rom. 8:35–39)

These words, perhaps more than any others ever penned, express the basis of our hope and comfort in this time of sorrow and grief.

God's Astounding Love

Paul begins with the simplest, most elemental truth of the Bible: God loves us. This in itself is amazing. We can understand how God might ignore us; we can understand how God might reject us, or even condemn us. But why and how He should love us is astounding.

F. M. Lehmen described God's love beautifully when he wrote,

> *The love of God is greater far*
> *Than tongue or pen can ever tell;*
> *It goes beyond the highest star,*
> *And reaches to the lowest hell . . .*
> *Oh, love of God, how rich and pure!*
> *How measureless and strong!*
> *It shall forevermore endure—*
> *The saints' and angels' song.*

God's love can be seen everywhere. Someone has said, "The mountains are God's love piled high; the oceans are God's love spread out; and the flowers are God's love in bloom"; but, the surest and purest expression of God's love is in the cross. Paul declares,

> For while *we were* still helpless, at the appointed moment, *Christ died for the ungodly. For* rarely will someone die *for a* just person—though for a good person someone might even dare to die. But God proves His own love for us in that while we were still sinners, Christ died for us! (Rom. 5:6–8, italics added)

In your sorrow, don't forget God loves you.

God's Surrounding Love

Second, God's love is all-encompassing. Paul declares that it covers every circumstance of life and that nothing can separate us from it. Paul asks, "Who can separate us from the love of Christ?" Then, before he answers his own question, he lists seven tragedies that might befall us, things commonly believed in his day to be signs of divine disfavor. These are things that might make us think God doesn't love us. Paul asks, "Can . . .

affliction

or

anguish

or

persecution

or

famine

or

nakedness

or

danger

or

sword?"

Then to his own question he gives a resounding, "No, in all these things we are more than victorious through Him who loved us" (Rom. 8:35–37).

Then, to reinforce this marvelous truth, Paul adds a series of ten contrasts. He writes, "I am persuaded [absolutely convinced] that

> not even death or life,
> angels or rulers,
> things present or things to come,
> height or depth,
> or any other created thing
> will have the power to separate us from
> the love of God
> that is in Christ Jesus our Lord! (vv. 38–39)

These things may separate us from health and wealth, from family and friends, from comfort and ease, but they cannot separate us from Christ.

Make special note of Paul's words, "Not even death or life" will separate us from the love of God. This means that our relationship with God does not depend upon the way we die any more than it depends on the way we live. It is all of His grace. God's love for us is not only astounding, it is surrounding.

God's Abounding Love

Finally, God's love is abounding. It makes us "more than victorious" in life. Because of His love we need not be overcome, whipped, or defeated by our circumstances. Rather, we can be overcomers through Him. He gives us strength and grace to stand up to life. He supplies inner braces for the outer pressures we experience.

The greatest enemies we face are sin, suffering, and death. Through Christ we can have victory over all three. We can have victory over sin through His death. We can have victory over suffering through His presence. We can have victory over death through His resurrection. As Paul declares, "[Jesus] has abolished death [rendered it powerless] and has brought life and immorality to light through the gospel" (2 Tim. 1:10).

An unknown poet has expressed our hope beautifully:

The stars shine down on the earth
The stars shine down on the sea
The stars shine on the face of God
The stars shine down on me.
The stars shall shine for a thousand years
For a thousand years and a day
But my Christ and I will still live on
When the stars have faded away.

Walter Winchell was a famous radio news commentator during World War II. Once, after a particularly dark week during which the port of Singapore fell, he closed his broadcast with this sentence: "Singapore has fallen, but the Rock of Ages stands."[1]

You probably feel as though your world has fallen today; but I remind you, the Rock of Ages stands. Christ lives and loves and lifts. He will strengthen and sustain you if you will look to Him. Nothing can ever separate you from His astounding, surrounding, and abounding love.[2]

Chapter 2

A Woman Who Needs No Eulogy

✳ Proverbs 31:30 ✳

WHEN ISABEL COLEMAN, longtime missionary to China, died, her memorial service was conducted by several of the people she had won to Christ. A Chinese man read a brief history of Miss Coleman's life in Chinese. When he concluded, he said in English, "For those who did not know Miss Coleman, no words are adequate to describe her life. For those who knew her, no words are necessary."

I feel that same way today. We are here to commemorate the life of a woman who needs no eulogy. When a person has lived such a godly life, there is nothing we can add to it. Her eulogy comes naturally and spontaneously from what she was and what she did.

The Bible teaches us this in its picture of the ideal woman in Proverbs 31:10–31. She is described as trustworthy, industrious, compassionate, and wise. Then it says,

Charm is deceptive, and beauty is fleeting, but a woman who fears the LORD will be praised. (Prov. 31:30)

This is the most important thing about her. She gives priority to the eternal and spiritual values of life. She fears God; that is, she has a deep reverence for and awe of God. She values Him above both charm and beauty. She knows that charm can be deceptive. It can cover up the real person. We are all such marvelous actors and actresses that we can fool people by our actions.

And she knows that beauty is fleeting. It is like the air we breathe. It quickly fades away. But God is eternal. A man said of Bess Truman, wife of former President Harry S. Truman, "Her values were deeper than cosmetics." That should be said of every Christian woman. The woman who reverences and worships Him shall be praised. Her praise, her eulogy, will come from the family she loved, the work she did, and the God she served.

Eulogized by Her Family

First, a godly woman is eulogized by her family. The writer of Proverbs says, "Her sons rise up and call her blessed. Her husband also praises her" (v. 28). A woman can have no greater eulogy than that of a loving family.

There is no greater argument for the Christian faith than that of a godly life. Someone has said, "One good mother is worth a hundred school teachers and an ounce of a mother is worth a pound of parson." The praise of a loving family is one of the greatest of all eulogies.

Eulogized by Her Works

Second, a godly woman is eulogized by the works she did. Again the writer of Proverbs says, "Give her the reward of her labor, and let her works praise her at the city gates" (Prov. 31:31).

The city gates in the Old Testament were equivalent to our city hall. It was the place where people met and transacted business. There a person was known for what he really was. Our works always reveal our true character. Our faith should show itself in the courthouse as well as the church house.

In one of his essays, Ralph Waldo Emerson said,

See how the mass of men worry themselves into nameless graves, while here and there a great unselfish soul forgets himself into immortality.

The Scriptures say of Jesus, "He went about doing good" (Acts 10:38). So should we.

A life of unselfish service is a eulogy in itself. Dorcas's life was an example of this kind of service. She was a disciple of Jesus Christ and a member of the early New Testament church. Her life was characterized by good works and deeds of mercy. When she died, her friends came to prepare her body for burial. Then someone remembered that the apostle Peter was nearby and sent for him with the hopes that he might be able to raise her from the dead.

When Peter arrived he found many widows standing around the body of Dorcas, weeping and holding coats and garments that she had made for them while she was alive. What she had done spoke of what she was. Her works eulogized her.

Her life is a beautiful example to all of us. It suggests that we all ought to be something—a disciple; do something—good works; and leave something—the memory of loving service. When we have lived a life of service, our good works are the only eulogy we need.

Eulogized by Her God

Third, a godly woman is eulogized by the Lord. That's what we have here in Proverbs 31. The eternal God who made the heavens and the earth pauses in this Scripture to praise this woman.

Every true follower of Christ can anticipate God's commendation. When we have loved God devotedly and followed Him faithfully, we can expect one day to hear Him say, "Well done, good and faithful servant" (Matt. 25:21 NKJV).

The Lord always knows who and what we are. The Scriptures say,

> For the eyes of Yahweh roam throughout the earth to show Himself strong for those whose hearts are completely His. (2 Chron. 16:9)

The Lord knew that Enoch walked with Him and did not hesitate to say that Enoch pleased Him (Heb. 11:5). The Lord knew that Abraham believed Him and did not hesitate to say that Abraham was His friend (James 2:23). The Lord knew that David loved Him and did not hesitate to say that David was a man after His own heart (Acts 13:22).

The Lord knows us, too. And He will gladly attest to our character in eternity. So, a godly woman really needs no eulogy. Her whole life is a eulogy. It speaks for itself. We cannot add to it nor take away from it.

Like the life of Miss Coleman, for those who did not know her, no words are adequate to describe her life. For those who did know her, no words are necessary.

Chapter 3

The Wonders of Heaven

✳ Revelation 21:1–4 ✳

IT HAS BEEN said, "People who die are so terribly gone except for those who see beyond sight and hear beyond sound."

"See beyond sight . . . hear beyond sound": How does one do that? Only through the Word of God.

John tells us in Revelation 21:1–4,

> Then I saw a new heaven and a new earth, for the first heaven and the first earth had passed away, and the sea no longer existed. I also saw the Holy City, new Jerusalem, coming down out of heaven from God, prepared like a bride adorned for her husband. Then I heard a loud voice from the throne:
> Look! God's dwelling is with humanity,
> and He will live with them.
> They will be His people,
> and God Himself will be with them,
> and be their God.
> He will wipe away every tear from their eyes.

Death will no longer exist;
grief, crying, and pain will exist no longer,
because the previous things have passed away.

Note those two phrases, "I saw . . ." and "I heard a voice . . ." John tells us that he saw beyond sight and he heard beyond sound, and what he saw and heard gave him hope, for he saw the wonders of heaven.

He saw and heard about three things that can help us through this time of grief: our mysteries will be cleared, our infirmities will be healed, and our redemption will be complete.

Our Mysteries Will Be Cleared

Life is full of things we simply do not understand. Some people enjoy vigorous health all of their lives, and some people are sick and frail from their youth. Some people die too soon, and some people live too long.

Some people have their driver's license taken away at an early age, and some seem to keep them forever. I have a friend who wrote me last Christmas and said, "I turn ninety-five next week and I just had my driver's license renewed for two more years." How would you like to meet her on a narrow highway late one night?

Franklin Delano Roosevelt, thirty-second president of the United States, was born to privilege. He was on the verge of a brilliant career when he was stricken with polio at the age of thirty-nine. For the next twenty-four years, until his death at age sixty-three, he walked with fourteen-pound braces on his legs or was pushed around in a wheelchair. We wonder why men like him suffered infirmities while Stalin and Hitler seemed to enjoy vigorous health.

For that matter, why is there cancer? Alzheimer's? Parkinson's? Multiple sclerosis? We simply do not know. But one day in heaven the mysteries will be cleared.

The apostle Paul writes in 1 Corinthians 13:12, "For now we see indistinctly, as in a mirror, but then face to face. Now I know in part, but then I will know fully, as I am fully known." That is our hope. One day we shall see clearly and will know fully.

Our Infirmities Will Be Healed

Richard Baxter was a good and godly pastor who spent years of his life in physical agony. His pain was intensified by the fact that he was in prison part of that time for preaching the gospel. Baxter was on his deathbed when a friend came to visit. He pulled a chair up to his bed and asked, "Richard, how are you doing?" And Richard replied, "Friend, I'm almost well." And then he died.

Will sickness and sorrow ever go away? Oh, yes, in heaven. There will be no blind eyes in heaven. No twisted limbs up there. No ambulances screaming down streets of gold. No funeral wreaths hanging on mansion doors. There will be no deaths, no sorrow, no pain, and no tears. For former things will have passed away, and He will make all things new.

When I visited a cemetery in Greenwood, Mississippi, years ago, I saw an epitaph on a tombstone that read, "Crippled on earth—made whole in heaven." That is our hope. Our infirmities will be healed.

Our Redemption Will Be Complete

When sin entered the world, all of creation fell under its curse—both environmental nature and human nature. There is no part of creation that was untouched by the ravages of sin. Today we are still under that curse and will remain so until our redemption is complete. The apostle Paul writes in Romans 8:22, "For we know that the whole creation has been groaning together with labor pains until now." Tornadoes, floods, earthquakes, and hurricanes are all the groans of nature longing for redemption.

Not just environmental nature but also human nature is under the curse of sin. Paul writes, "We groan in this body (i.e., from the burdens of life)" (2 Cor. 5:2). We all experience aches, pains, trials, and tribulations. Age guarantees that we will have groans. Our redemption was settled at Calvary. On the cross Jesus said, "It is finished!" (John 19:30). He did not say, "I am finished." He was far from finished and He is still alive and at work in the world today, but we will not realize the full effects of His redemption until we get to heaven.

I have a friend whose grandson was born prematurely. For several weeks the child held on to the slender thread of life. When the thread gave way and the child died, the chaplain at the hospital called my friend to give him a word of comfort. But before the chaplain could say anything, my friend said to him, "At least he has gone to a better place." The chaplain replied, "No, no—he has not gone to a better place. He has gone to the best place." That is our hope and the wonder of heaven.

18

Chapter 4

When Is a Person
Ready to Die?

✳ Luke 2:25–32 ✳

RETIRED MISSIONARY DR. Harry Schweinsberg and I talked once about the death of a mutual friend. Harry had been on a mission trip in Mexico when our friend died. The family wanted Harry to participate in the funeral service, so he returned home immediately. As they journeyed, one of Harry's traveling companions asked him if he was afraid to die. He responded, "No, not in the least. But I am afraid of living too long."

There are times when a sick person longs for relief, like a tired person longs for rest. Most people who suffer constant and excruciating pain or have lost mental faculties may prefer what they consider an alternative.

Whether death comes in youth or old age, suddenly, or after a prolonged illness, the important thing is that a person be ready to die. If we are ready to die regardless of the circumstances, we can die in peace.

When is a person ready to die? When can a person die in peace?

The Bible gives us an example in the life of Simeon. When Jesus was but eight days old, His parents brought Him to the temple in Jerusalem and they placed Him in the arms of an aged priest named Simeon to be dedicated to God.

Simeon was a godly man who lived in expectancy of the coming Savior. The Holy Spirit had revealed to him in some way that he would not die until he had seen the Messiah.

When Simeon took the baby Jesus in his arms, he blessed God and said, "Lord, now You are letting Your servant depart in peace, according to Your word; for my eyes have seen Your salvation" (Luke 2:29–30 NKJV).

Simeon's experience teaches us that you are ready to "die in peace" if these three things are in place.

When You Have Lived a Faithful Life

Simeon was a faithful man of God, described as "righteous and devout." Since he lived in expectancy of the coming Messiah, "the Holy Spirit was on him" (Luke 2:25).

Someone has said, "One must be a wide-awake Christian before he can fall 'asleep in Jesus.'" This is not to suggest that we are saved by our good life. No. Our salvation is never based on our goodness but on His grace. If we are saved, we should live in such a way that we won't be ashamed to face Him (1 John 2:28).

The Scriptures say, "It is expected of managers that each one of them be found faithful" (1 Cor. 4:2). We are not told to be faithful until we are tired, or until we are retired, but until we are expired. We are to be faithful unto death.

When we have lived faithfully and obediently, we can then die in peace.

When Your Life's Work Is Complete

We know nothing about Simeon beyond this experience. He enters the pages of Scripture for a brief moment, plays a bit part in the drama of redemption, and then exits to be heard from no more. So far as we know, he never wrote a book, never led a great movement, or ever made a memorable speech. Apparently he was content to serve God in obscurity.

Scripture does not articulate how, but it was revealed to Simeon by the Holy Spirit that he would not die until he saw the Messiah. When the baby Jesus was placed in his arms, he immediately recognized and acknowledged Him as the Savior and then disappeared from the scene as quickly as he had come.

It was as if he was born for this purpose, for this moment, for this one act. And once it was done, his life's work was over.

I believe God has a purpose, a will, for every one of us. We are not here by accident. Our coming was no surprise to Him. Every great person in the Bible lived with this confidence and died with the satisfaction that he had done God's will.

Mark Twain said, "The two most important days in your life are the day you were born and the day you find out why."

Jesus said, "My food is to do the will of Him who sent Me and to finish His work" (John 4:34). On the cross He declared, "It is finished!" (John 19:30). He did not say, "I am finished." He said, "It [God's plan] is finished!" Jesus lived His life under the conviction and died with the satisfaction that He had done the will of God.

It was the same with the apostle Paul. His primary concern in life was not his personal safety and ease, but that he finish the course God had for him (Acts 20:24). At the end of his life he said, "I have finished the race . . ." (2 Tim. 4:7). Paul, like Jesus, lived with the conviction and died with the satisfaction that he had done God's will.

At a meeting of the Fellowship of Christian Athletes, Bobby Richardson, former New York Yankee second baseman, offered a prayer that ought to express the desire of every believer. It is a classic in brevity and poignancy: "Dear God, Your will, nothing more, nothing less, nothing else. Amen."

If we've lived our lives by the will of God, when our life's work is done, we can die in peace.

When Jesus Is Your Savior and Lord

When Simeon saw the baby Jesus, he immediately recognized who He was and said, "My eyes have seen Your salvation" (Luke 2:30).

With deep spiritual insight, Simeon confessed his faith in Christ. Notice how he described Him:

- He is the anointed of God (v. 26).
- He is the light of the Gentiles (v. 32).
- He is the glory of Israel (v. 32).
- He is the hope of mankind (v. 31).
- He is the Savior of the world (vv. 31–32).

That's the recognition and confession every person needs to make.

James Jeffrey, former all-American football player and a leader in the Fellowship of Christian Athletes, spoke at one of Baylor University's homecoming activities. A few months earlier he had learned he had cancer of the pancreas. The doctor had given him less than a year to live. As he spoke to us that night, the ravages of his cancer were already evident in his once strong body. In his testimony he said, "I've told people all my life, 'Jesus is all you need,' but you never know Jesus is all you need until you get to the place where He is all you've got. When He's all you've got, then you know He's all you need."

To acknowledge and receive Christ as personal Savior is the best and only spiritual preparation for death. Until that has been done, no person is ready to die; but once you have done that, you can die in peace.

"The time for my departure is close. I have fought the good fight, I have finished the race, I have kept the faith" (2 Tim. 4:6–7).

Chapter 5

Death from the Other Side

✳ Psalm 116:15 ✳

I HAD AN early-morning flight out of Memphis, Tennessee, several years ago. It was one of those dreary mornings when the clouds hung like a dirty sponge over the earth. It looked as if you could reach up and squeeze the water out of them. The ceiling was so low I wondered if we could take off. But about twelve hundred feet up we broke through the clouds into the most beautiful sunlight I have ever seen.

The sun, you know, is always shining above. But sometimes here below it is obscured by the clouds. As I looked down on the clouds below, the earth appeared to be covered with a blanket of snow. They looked like the backs of ten thousand sheep racing across the sky. As I sat looking down at them, I realized I was looking at the same clouds that I had seen below. The difference was I was seeing them from the other side, from heaven's side. From below they looked dark and foreboding. From above they looked beautiful and peaceful. They were the same clouds, only from the other side.

A few years ago my sister became interested in making rag rugs. From the topside, her rugs were beautiful tapestries. But from the backside, they were a maze of knots, unraveled edges, and loose strings. The same rug, but viewed from the other side.

Heaven is like that. A little girl was taking an evening walk with her father. She looked up at the starry night sky and wonderingly exclaimed, "Oh, Daddy, if the wrong side of heaven is so beautiful, what must the right side be!"

Death is like that for the one who trusts Christ. It looks different from the other side. The psalmist expressed this truth when he wrote, "The death of His faithful ones is valuable in the LORD's sight" (Ps. 116:15). Mark that phrase, "in the LORD's sight." That's the key. In our sight, the death of God's faithful ones appears tragic. In His sight, it is precious and valuable. That's the difference in death from the other side.

From this side, for us, death is a time of sorrow, of loss, of defeat, and of separation. But from the other side, for them, it is a time of release, of reunion, of rest, and of reward.

One man about whom I read had the right spirit, for he said to his dying mother, "I'm going to let you go now, Mother. Have a good time. You have waited long for this joy."

Too often we think of death as coming to destroy everything for which we have lived. We should picture death as coming to save those we love. Many times we think of death as the end; rather, we should think of death as the beginning. We often think of losing, when it should be gain. We think of parting instead of arrival. It is not closing the door of life; it is opening the gate to eternity.

We who hope in Christ would do well today to look at death from the other side. In fact, we might glean four comforting truths from this perspective:

From this side, death looks like the end; from the other side, it is the beginning.

When you look at death from this side, it seems so final. It appears to be the end of life, the end of relationships, the end of all that we have worked for, all that we have earned, all that we have laid up. But, from the other side, death is not the end; it's an entrance. It is not a goal, but a gateway. It is the beginning of a bright new life—eternal life for the believer in Jesus Christ.

Some anonymous writer comes nearest to describing this view of death in what he called "The Ship":

> I am standing upon the seashore. A ship at my side spreads her white sails in the morning breeze and starts for the blue ocean. She is an object of beauty and strength, and I stand and watch her until at length she is only a ribbon, or a white cloud, just where the sea and sky come to mingle with each other.
>
> Then someone at my side says: "There! She's gone!"
>
> Gone? Where? Gone from my sight, that's all. She is just as large in mast and hull and spar as she was when she left my side, and just as able to bear her load of living freight—to the place of destination. Her

diminished size is in me, not in her; and just at the moment when someone at my side says, "There! She's gone!" there are other voices ready to take up the glad shout. "There! She comes!"

And that is the saint's dying.

That's good, really good! And the Scriptures confirm it. Paul speaks of his own death as "a departure" (2 Tim. 4:6). The word *depart* is a nautical term that means to weigh anchor and set sail. Rightly understood, then, death is not the end. It is the beginning of a new life.

From this side, death looks like separation; from the other side, it is reunion.

The Scriptures describe death in various ways. It is spoken of as a departure—weighing anchor and setting sail; as an exodus—a going out; as a dissolution—taking down one's earthly tent and moving on. But my favorite description is when the Scriptures say of Abraham, "He took his last breath . . . and was gathered to his people" (Gen. 25:8).

The expression, "gathered to his people," clearly implies something more than being carried back to the old family cemetery or being buried in a common tomb or vault. It has a deeper and more spiritual meaning than that. Abraham was convinced of joining his deceased loved ones in fellowship and personal association. It suggests, I believe, that he became a part of a glad reunion that is a part of our Christian hope (1 Thess. 4:13–18).

A story I heard many years ago beautifully illustrates this hope. An elderly Christian woman was grief-stricken after the death of her daughter. To adjust, she boarded a ship from England to New York City to visit her other daughter. While at sea a severe storm struck. Passengers frantically raced for lifeboats. The elderly Christian lady showed no signs of panic. A young man excitedly said, "Lady, don't you know we may sink and all die!"

"Young man," she quietly replied, "I have a daughter in heaven and a daughter in New York City, and it doesn't make any difference to me which one I go to see."

This hope makes heaven even more wonderful than it would be otherwise. In the words of poet, James Whitcomb Riley, who lost a little child in death, in the poem "She Is Just Away,"

> *I cannot say, and I will not say,*
> *That she is dead: she's just away!*
> *With a cheery smile and a wave of the hand,*
> *She has wandered into a better land.*
> *And left us dreaming how very fair*
> *It needs must be, since she lingers there.*

Clearly, from the other side, death is not the end; it is the beginning. It is not parting; it is arrival. It is not separation; it is reunion. When two people are Christians, they never say good-bye for the last time.

**From this side, death looks like a loss;
from the other side, it is gain.**

Somerset Maugham said, "Death is a very dull, dreary affair, and my advice to you is to have nothing whatsoever to do with it." In contrast to that dreary view of death is that of the apostle Paul, who said, "For me, living is Christ, but dying is gain" (Phil. 1:21). The word *gain* is a business term that means "to make a profit." The bottom line is, death is not losing; it is gaining. For the Christian, it is a paying proposition.

A minister reading the Bible to a suffering hospital patient quoted from Revelation 21:4, ". . . grief, crying, and pain will exist no longer." From jaws clenched in agony came the reply, "Won't that be wonderful—no more pain!"

I love the story of Richard Baxter, a good and godly preacher who spent his last several years (and I use the plural) in physical agony. His pain was intensified by the fact that he was imprisoned for preaching the gospel. Shortly before his death, a friend visited with him. The friend pulled his chair up next to Richard's bed and said to the great preacher, "Richard, how are you doing?" And Richard replied, "Friend, I am almost well." And he died. Think of that, "I am almost well." And then he died.

**From this side, death appears to be defeat;
from the other side, it is victory.**

Death has been swallowed up in victory. Death, where is your victory? Death, where is your sting? (1 Cor. 15:54–55)

There is a glorious absence of fear in Christian funerals. The finality of death is offset by the finished work of the cross. The wonderful truth of the Bible is, the moment we close our eyes in death, we open them in glory.

So remember, "The death of His faithful ones is valuable in the LORD's sight" (Ps. 116:15), and "weeping may spend the night, but there is joy in the morning" (Ps. 30:5). What happens in the morning? In the morning we will be healthy. In the morning we will be happy. And in the morning we will be home. That's death from the other side.

Chapter 6

Well Done

✳ Luke 2:36–38 ✳

ON THE OCCASION of Dwight D. Eisenhower's one hundred birthday anniversary (March 27, 1990), his son, John S. D. Eisenhower, in a speech before the joint session of Congress closed by saying, "Ike is now a part of history, gone from us for twenty-one years tomorrow, and one single line of the West Point alma mater comes to mind. The words read, 'And when our work is done, our course is run, may it be said, "well done: be thou our peace."'"

Then he closed the speech by saying, "This is the way that Dwight Eisenhower would like to be remembered by those he left behind."[3]

We come today to say good-bye to a friend with those same words, "Well done: be thou our peace."

In many ways, I think the life of our friend parallels the life of Anna, a prophetess mentioned in the New Testament. She's introduced to us in three short verses in the Gospel of Luke. We know nothing about her except what is recorded

33

here. She makes an entrance on the stage of Christian history, plays a bit part, and then makes her exit, never to be heard from again. But what Luke tells us in this passage of Scripture gives us insight into the character of this saintly woman.

Anna was a widow eighty-four years of age. She had married early in life, and after seven years of marriage her husband died. She did not allow that experience to embitter her but remained a faithful servant and worshiper of the Lord the rest of her life. She lived in an area around the temple and daily went there to pray and to render whatever service she could to the house of God.

According to the Law of Moses, Jesus' parents brought Him to the temple to dedicate Him to the Lord (Lev. 12; Luke 2:22). When they handed the baby to the aged priest, Simeon, he said, "Lord, now You are letting Your servant depart in peace . . . for my eyes have seen Your salvation" (Luke 2:29–30 NKJV). At that moment Anna came near and, hearing his decree, began to sing praises to the Lord and to tell everyone she met that their hopes and dreams of a Savior had finally come true (vv. 36–38). I chose this experience from the Scriptures because the life of Anna and the life of our friend teach us about life and death.

Consider some of these lessons: We can experience sorrow without becoming bitter; we can grow old without losing hope; we can die without fear.

We Can Experience Sorrow without Becoming Bitter

Anna had been married to her husband only seven years when he died. He could not have been very old, and I'm sure she wanted to ask God, "Why?" But she did not allow her sorrow to cause her to become bitter or a quitter in life. She knew that God was her Father and that the Father's hand will never cause a child a needless tear.

Life deals some people a hard blow. Sicknesses, sorrows, and hardships come to all of us. They can make us bitter or they can make us better. The choice is ours. When in his old age he lost his beloved daughter, Bishop Darlington said, "I feel like an old tree, standing out in the field, struck many times by lightning. This last bolt has shattered me. But I'm still standing. My face is toward the sunrise and with good hope I face the future."

Nothing can destroy a person like the loss of a loved one in death. But a faith in Christ like Anna's and our friend's can enable us to sing in the midst of the storm and still praise through the prism of a tear.

Karen Kingsbury helps us set things in perspective when she writes, "We never own the people in our lives. We love them but they are on loan from God. We can have them for a moment and then they are gone. Grieve because you miss them. And we will. But don't get mad at God for the minutes you will miss with them. Thank God for the minutes you had."[4]

Develop that attitude of gratitude and it will save you from bitterness at life's losses. Thank God that neither Anna nor our friend allowed their sorrow to make them become bitter or a quitter in life.

We Can Grow Old without Losing Hope

Growing old is one of the few things that comes to us without effort. It just happens.

Early in my ministry a church was interested in me and I was interested in the church. Word came that they thought I was too young. So I visited with an older, experienced minister, Grady Metcalf, to talk to him about my situation.

I said, "Grady, they're interested in me, but they feel I am too young." Grady responded, "Paul, if that's your only problem, time will take care of it." Well, it has. It's been a long time since I've been asked to lead a youth revival. I always intended to grow old, but not this soon.

Aging can be hard on our faith. The years and the tears and the fears of life can sap the vitality from our hopes and dreams. How do we grow old without growing stale? How do we keep hope alive?

Even Billy Graham, nearing the age of ninety, granted one of his last interviews. He said, "As a Christian I know how to die but nobody ever taught me how to grow old."[5]

Anna and our friend give us some insight. Anna kept her hopes alive by faithfully serving God through the house of worship and daily prayer. The church is God's gift to us. We cheat ourselves if we neglect it. Fellowship with God's people strengthens our hope. And prayer is a privilege. Think of it: We can talk to the maker of heaven and earth about any problem in our life. Prayer along with faithful worship helps to keep hope alive. It did for Anna. It did for our friend. It will for you and me.

We Can Die without Fear

Though the Scriptures do not say that specifically about Anna, because her faith was firmly planted in the Savior she joyfully proclaimed, we know it was true. Like Simeon, the priest, she could say, "Now [let] Your servant depart in peace, . . . for my eyes have seen Your salvation" (Luke 2:29–30 NKJV).

Though our friend and Anna both grew old and frail in body, their faith continued to be young and vibrant because it was centered in Jesus, the Savior, the Messiah, the Promised One of God who came to redeem us.

And our friend, like Anna, freely confessed Him and followed Him. We should do the same.

I close as I began with Dwight D. Eisenhower. His grandfather was a minister in the River Brethren Church. The tombstone of his aunt Lillia, who died at the age of seventeen, reads:

She gave her heart to Jesus
Who took her stains away
But now in Christ believing
the Father too can say
I'm going home to glory
A golden crown to wear
O meet me, meet me over there.

That's what we all need to do. We need to give our hearts to Jesus and prepare to meet our loved ones "over there."

Chapter 7

Faith to Go On

✳ John 14:1–6 ✳

DR. KENNETH MCFARLAND, in one of his motivational speeches, told of an item he found on the obituary page of the newspaper in a small Southern town. It read, "Billy, it was just a year ago today that you left us and the sunshine went out of our lives. But we turned on the headlights and we're going on . . . and, Billy, we shall keep on doing the best we can until that glorious day when we shall see you again."

It was signed simply, "Love, the family." No names, just a simple confession of faith—the kind of faith that enables a person to go on in the face of sorrow and death.

When a person loses a loved one in death as you have, we need the same kind of faith as this family, the kind of faith that turns on the headlights and goes on in the dark hours of sorrow.

Jesus gave us the ingredients of that kind of faith when He said,

"Your heart must not be troubled. Believe in God; believe also in Me. In my Father's house are many dwelling places; if not, I would have told you. I am going away to prepare a place for you. If I go away and prepare a place for you, I will come back and receive you to Myself, so that where I am, you may be also. You know the way to where I am going." "Lord," Thomas said, "we don't know where You're going. How can we know the way?" Jesus told him, "I am the way, the truth, and the life. No one comes to the Father except through Me." (John 14:1–6)

The occasion for these words was Jesus announcing to the apostles that He must go away (i.e., He would soon die).

This was devastating news to them. They had left all to follow Him. For three years they had built their lives around Him. Their hopes and dreams centered on Him. Now, He said He was going away.

Naturally, they were perplexed. How could they go on? How could they continue without Him? Then, as if to tell them how, He gave them and us the ingredients of a strong and sustaining faith.

It involves three things: faith in a person, faith in a place, and faith in a promise. Jesus was saying, we can go on in spite of our sorrow and loss if we believe in Jesus as our Savior, if we believe in heaven as our home, and if we believe in the return of Christ as our hope.

We Can Go On If Jesus Is Our Savior

Jesus said, "Believe in God; believe also in Me" (14:1). It is one thing to believe in God; only believing in Jesus legitimizes that profession. Muslims profess to believe in God. They say, "There is no God but Allah, and Mohammed is his prophet." Deists profess to believe in God. They say that He created the world, wound it up like a giant clock, and left it to run itself.

So, to profess to believe in God may mean that you simply believe in a power that creates. To believe in Jesus means you believe in a personal God who saves.

The Bible declares, "For God loved the world in this way: He gave His One and Only Son, so that everyone who believes in Him will not perish, but have eternal life" (John 3:16). Believing in His love and care can keep us going.

A pastor friend told me a story that displays this truth. Early in his ministry he and a member of his church worked together in a number of revival meetings. He did the preaching; his friend led the music.

His friend began to have throat problems and checked into a hospital for tests. The results revealed he had throat cancer.

The man's wife called the pastor to the hospital. When he arrived, she told him the diagnosis and said, "My husband doesn't know. I need you to help me tell him."

When they walked into the hospital room, the layman said to his wife, "Honey, why don't you get us a Coke? I imagine the pastor is thirsty. We can drink while we talk."

When she was gone, the layman said to his pastor, "Preacher, I know I've got cancer and they don't know how to tell me. But it's okay. All these years we've been telling people Jesus is enough. Now He is going to give me a chance to prove it."

Sometime later, just before he died, the layman said to my friend, "Pastor, wherever you go, as long as you live, you can tell people Jesus is true to His Word. Jesus is enough."

J. Wilbur Chapman's hymn "Jesus! What a Friend of Sinners!" expresses what faith in Jesus does for us.

> *Jesus! What a help in sorrow!*
> *While the billows o'er me roll*
> *Even when my heart is breaking,*
> *He, my comfort, helps my soul*
> *Hallelujah! What a savior!*
> *Hallelujah! What a friend!*
> *Saving, helping, keeping, loving,*
> *He is with me to the end.*

That's how belief in Jesus gives us the faith to go on.

We Can Go On If Heaven Is Our Home

Carl Sandburg, in his book *Abraham Lincoln: The Prairie Years and the War Years*, tells of the hardships endured by the early pioneers in Illinois who were contemporaries of Abraham Lincoln. Life was hard and death was common. Nancy Hanks, Lincoln's mother, lost one child and later died herself. It was said that a fourth of all babies died within their first year.

Sandburg said the one bright spot in their otherwise bleak lives came when they gathered in their crude log churches each Lord's Day to worship. They sang and prayed and usually a circuit-riding Baptist or Methodist minister was there to preach to them.

As they worshiped, they could look out the windows of their little church and see new mounds of dirt—the graves of their loved ones who had died. And one of the songs they sang was "There's a Land That Is Fairer Than Day":

> *There's a land that is fairer than day*
> *And by faith we can see it afar,*
> *For the Father waits over the way*
> *To prepare us a dwelling place there.*
>
> *In the sweet by and by,*
> *We shall meet on that beautiful shore,*
> *In the sweet by and by,*
> *We shall meet on that beautiful shore.*
>
> Sanford F. Bennett

Life for my grandparents was not much different. When I was a boy I used to visit them each summer, and while there I attended their little Missionary Baptist church deep in the backwoods of east Texas. The one-room frame building was lighted with Coleman lanterns, the pews were homemade slat benches, and the men sat on one side, the women on the other. Much of their music was about heaven. I now understand why.

Life was hard and the people were poor in those days. They had few of this world's goods and little hope of things getting better. Heaven was the only real hope they had for a better life. One of the songs I remember in particular was A. S. Bridgewater's "How Beautiful Heaven Must Be."

How beautiful heaven must be
sweet home of the ransomed and free
Bright hope for the end of life's journey
How beautiful heaven must be.

It was that faith that kept them going, and it keeps us going also.

I am sometimes asked, "What is heaven like?" In the words of R. G. Lee, "It is the most beautiful place the mind of God could conceive and the hand of God could create." The apostle John described it as "a bride adorned for her husband" (Rev. 21:2).

A young lady is seldom more beautiful than on her wedding day. Usually more money and more time and more planning goes into that appearance than any other of her life. When she stands at the altar with her bridegroom, she is the personification of purity and beauty.

That's what heaven is like.

We Can Go On If the Return of Christ Is Our Hope

What happens to a person at death? Death is defined in Scripture as a separation of the spirit from the body (James 2:26). At death, the body is buried in the ground where it will remain until the resurrection, and the spirit of the Christian returns to the Lord to await the resurrection.

The apostle Paul, speaking of death, said we will be "out of the body and at home with the Lord" (2 Cor. 5:8). Jesus, as He died on the cross, said, "Father, into Your hands I entrust My spirit" (Luke 23:46). His body was buried in Joseph's tomb, but His Spirit went to the Father. Three days later His Spirit reinhabited His body and He was raised from the dead.

Just so, one day the trumpet of God shall sound, and Christ shall return to the earth in power and glory. When that occurs, the first thing that will happen is the dead in Christ will be raised. Their spirits, which have been with the Lord, will reinhabit their new resurrected bodies. Then we who are alive and remain, shall be caught up together with them in the air. Thereafter we shall live eternally with Him in our new and glorified bodies, free of disease and no longer subject to decay and death (1 Thess. 4:16).

What will our resurrection bodies be like? Our burial is sometimes referred to as a planting. In the springtime, farmers and gardeners everywhere break up the soil in their fields and gardens and bury seeds in them. In time, the tiny seeds, watered by the rain and warmed by the sun, sprout and grow. From out of their earthly graves little plants poke their heads into the sunlight. Then they grow into beautiful flowers or fruit.

As the plant that comes out of the earth is far more glorious than the seed that was placed in the ground, so our resurrection bodies will be far more glorious than the dead bodies we bury in the grave. Our resurrection bodies will be like Christ's resurrection body. They will be glorious, transcendent, and recognizable.

The hope of our resurrection and eternal life rests solely in His return. That's why His return is called the "blessed hope" of believers (Titus 2:13). That's why belief in the return of Christ keeps us going.

Jesus summarized His teaching and our everlasting hope by saying, "I am the way, the truth, and the life. No one comes to the Father except through Me" (John 14:6).

> *Jesus is the way—without Him, there is no going.*
> *Jesus is the truth—without Him, there is no knowing.*
> *Jesus is the life—without Him, there is no growing.*

Put your faith in Him and you can go on.

Chapter 8

Things We Can Count On

✳ Revelation 21:5–8 ✳

PHILIP YANCEY, IN one of his writings, says,

> My father-in-law, a lifelong Bible teacher with strong
> Calvinistic roots, found his faith troubled in his final
> years. A degenerative nerve disease confined him to
> bed, impeding him from most of the activities that
> gave him pleasure. His thirty-nine-year-old daughter
> battled a severe form of diabetes. Financial pressures
> mounted. During the most severe crisis, he composed
> a Christmas letter and mailed it to others in the fam-
> ily. Many things that he had once taught he now felt
> uneasy about. What could he believe with certainty?
> He came up with these three things: "Life is difficult.
> God is merciful. Heaven is sure." These things he
> could count on when his daughter died of diabetes
> complications the very next week; he clung to those
> truths even more fiercely.[6]

There are some things in life we can count on. The risen Christ in Revelation 21:5 told John, "Write, because these words are faithful and true"—that is, they can be relied on to come to pass. There are some things we can know for sure. These certainties of Yancey's father-in-law are as true for us as they were for him: Life is difficult, God is merciful, and heaven is sure.

Life Is Difficult

Years ago I served on an insurance board in Des Moines, Iowa, and worked with a group of people of Norwegian descent. In a meeting one of them gave me a Norwegian saying, "Life is hard. If it isn't, it should be." We know from our own experience that it is. Suffering, accidents, disappointments, reversals, and old age come to all of us.

Years ago a young college student came home for a weekend and was killed in an automobile accident just a few blocks from his home. His parents were members of my congregation, and as I visited with them in preparation for the service, the brokenhearted father said, "Preacher, we're not supposed to bury our children; they're supposed to bury us." I'm not sure life is always the way it's supposed to be, but that's the way it is.

Job, who was no stranger to trouble, wrote, "But mankind is born for trouble as surely as sparks fly upward" (Job 5:7). And he wrote again, "Man born of woman is short of days, and full of trouble" (Job 14:1). Jesus reminds us, "You will have suffering . . . Be courageous! I have conquered the world"

(John 16:33). The late Carlyle Marney expressed it best when he said, "The problem is, life just won't lie down and behave."

Being a Christian does not alter that. Bill Reynolds, retired professor of Church Music at Southwestern Seminary, wrote more than seven hundred songs. He said he does not sing the hymn, "Everyday with Jesus Is Sweeter Than the Day Before" because it is not true. He says he is much more in sympathy with the lyrics from the spiritual "Nobody Knows the Trouble I've Seen": "Sometimes I'm up, sometimes I'm down . . . but still my soul is heaven bound." Then he would add, "We ought to sing the truth as well as tell the truth."

When in his old age, Bishop John Darlington lost his beloved daughter. He said, "I feel like an old tree, standing out in a field, struck many times by lightning. The last bolt has shattered me but I'm still standing. My face is toward the sunrise and with good hope in my heart I'm looking to the future."

If the thunderbolts of life have shattered you, we need to face it: life is hard.

God Is Merciful

It's hard to see that today. We know that only by faith.

A few years ago there was a garden in our city that covered the entire front yard of a person's home. There apparently was no design, no order, no pattern in the planting of the flowers. It was, in fact, a confused mess. A rock at the edge of the garden had inscribed on it, "God's Garden." As we passed one day I said to my wife, "That's not God's garden. He didn't design it; He is not the author of confusion. But He did make the flowers grow."

Sickness and death are products of the fall, but God can bring good and beauty out of tragedy just as He did that garden.

The Scriptures say, "We know that all things work together for the good of those who love God: those who are called according to His purpose" (Rom. 8:28). This verse is one of the keys to understanding God's work in today's world. It doesn't say that everything that happens is good—it isn't. It doesn't say that God causes everything that happens—He doesn't. It doesn't say that everything is going to work out well for everybody—it won't. It says rather that He can take the good and the bad—all things that happen—and make something good out of them. If we are His, we can trust that God is working in the bad as well as the good that happens to us so that we will become more like His Son, Jesus Christ.

Robert Zheore, pastor of Hope Lutheran Church in Stanton, Michigan, noted in 1997, "A deathbed is a hard place to teach faith. It is much better learned day by day, week by week."

He wrote of an elderly woman in his church: "When I last saw her, she was in the hospital bed that she would not leave alive. The last words I spoke to her were 3,400 years older than she. 'The LORD bless you and keep you; the LORD make His face shine upon you And be gracious to you; The LORD lift up His countenance upon you, and give you peace' (Num. 6:24–26 NKJV). She knew He would. The last word I heard her say was to God: 'Amen.'"

Heaven Is Real

We know that by faith. We know it because God said so and His words are "faithful and true" (Rev. 21:5)—they can be relied upon to come to pass.

What is heaven like? The great preacher of another generation R. G. Lee said, "It's the most beautiful place the mind of God could conceive and the hand of God could create." John, the apostle, describes it for us as "a bride adorned for her husband" (Rev. 21:2).

A young lady is never more beautiful than on her wedding day. In all probability, more effort, more attention, and more money have gone into that appearance than any other in her lifetime. And when she appears at the head of the aisle ready to walk down on the arm of her father and be presented to her groom, she is the personification of purity and beauty.

It is no accident that John uses that illustration to help us understand the beauty and wonder of heaven.

In John 14:2 Jesus speaks of it in this way: "In My Father's house are many dwelling places." A few years ago I was in a revival meeting in the little community of Mertens, Texas. While visiting in the home of one of the members for lunch one day, I read this inscription on the mantel above the fireplace: "In my Father's house are many mansions. I hope yours is next to mine."

That's the hope we have in Christ. That's one of the things about which we can be certain. The apostle Paul wrote the same sentiment to young Timothy: "I know the One I have believed in and am persuaded that He is able to guard what has been entrusted to me until that day" (2 Tim. 1:12).

So do I. So, while I know that life is hard, I have absolute confidence that God is merciful and that heaven is real. I have staked my life on that.

Chapter 9

All Things through Christ

✳ Philippians 4:13 ✳

WILLIAM WILBERFORCE, THE great British Reformer statesman, while a member of Parliament, became a committed Christian. It was partly through the influence of John Newton, a man he had admired since boyhood and the author of the great hymn "Amazing Grace."

As a Christian he contemplated giving up politics, but Newton persuaded him that he could serve Christ in the political arena effectively. In 1787, Wilberforce, after visiting with Newton, wrote in his diary: "God has set before me two great objects, the suppression of the slave trade and the reformation of manners [morals] in the British Empire."

It was no easy matter. Every year for twenty years he made a motion before Parliament for the abolition of slavery. Again and again it was defeated. Finally, on the night of February 23, 1807, three days before he died, the law was passed to abolish slavery.

In the latter years of his life, Wilberforce, like all of us do from time to time, went through periods of great despondency and was liable at times to suffer periods of melancholy. As his life neared an end, he said to his younger son, Henry, "I am at a very distressed state."

Henry replied gently, "Yes, Father, but you have your feet on the rock."

In times like these, nothing helps us quite as much as having our feet on the solid rock—Jesus Christ. It is our faith and trust in Him that can carry us through the difficult experiences of life.

I've preached and taught and counseled for over half a century, but I'm still mystified in the ways of life, death, and suffering. I do not know why young men are often cut off in the very prime of life. I do not know why faithful Christians suffer debilitating diseases. I will tell you what I do know: whatever happens to us or why ever it happens, God's grace is sufficient to see us through. The apostle Paul gives affirmation to this when he writes, "I am able to do all things through Him who strengthens me" (Phil. 4:13).

This is no flippant boast by the apostle Paul. When he wrote these words he was in prison in Rome awaiting trial for his life. He was chained to a Roman guard twenty-four hours a day. Incarceration restricted the great missionary work that God had called him to do. In addition, many of his friends had deserted him. After all, he was being tried as an insurrectionist. He was accused of being a ringleader for a band of rebels, and they did not want to be identified with him for fear of their own lives. All of this added to the pain of his chains.

Moreover, he was staring death in the face every day. The uncertainty of knowing whether he would live or die likely weighed heavily on his mind. His grief was compounded by the fact that a friend who had come to Philippi to assist him became seriously ill and almost died (Phil. 2:25–30).

In the midst of all of this, he wrote these triumphant words: "I am able to do all things through Him who strengthens me" (Phil. 4:13). There is nothing superficial or fragile about this great affirmation. The powerful truth of Scripture is that we can do all things through Christ also. The power and strength that was available to the apostle Paul is available to us today.

I'm not sure what he includes in the "all things" he was able to do, but let me suggest at least three: through Christ we can survive the loss of a loved one, endure years of suffering and illness, and face death triumphantly.

Surviving the Loss of a Loved One

First, through Christ we can survive the loss of a loved one—a husband, a son, a grandfather, and a friend. The apostle Paul knew what it was to suffer loss. Epaphroditus, the friend who came from the church at Philippi to assist him, became critically ill. Paul describes his condition as "nigh" unto death (Phil. 2:27 KJV). The word literally means "next door neighbor to." Epaphroditus was as near to death as a person could possibly get. While God did spare him rather than add sorrow on top of sorrow to Paul's plight, he did lose other missionary companions. He knew what death was like.

In the 1994 film *Forrest Gump*, when he lost his sweetheart, Forrest said, "Momma always said that death is a part of life. I sure wish it wasn't." Me too; but it is, and we must face it.

It can be a harrowing experience. A friend lost his wife of fifty-six years to Alzheimer's. He wrote, "My darling died three years ago today, and I tell you from experience that grief does not lessen. I did the best I could to care for my wife in her cruel illness, but I believe her Lord was good to take her when her body broke down and there was only confusion, fear, and pain left for her."

My friend further commented, "It is my empty house, my empty bed, and my empty arms that continue to hurt me so. Death has no terror for me. And, while I do not seek it, I would not flee it."

Madame De Staël said, "We understand death the first time when he puts his hand upon one whom we love." My friend learned that firsthand.

Sorrow is real but so is grace. Because of Christ we can endure the loss of a loved one.

Enduring Years of Suffering and Illness

Second, through Christ we can endure years of sickness and pain. If death is a mystery, suffering is more so. The apostle Paul experienced both. Philippians 4 speaks of his "afflictions." The words suggest both pressure and pain that he was called to endure.

In one of his other writings he speaks of having "a thorn in the flesh" (2 Cor. 12:7). The word *thorn* suggests that his affliction was intensely painful. The word *flesh* locates it. So Paul endured an intensely painful bodily affliction. He says that three times he banged on the doors of heaven asking God for relief, but it did not come.

The Lord's answer was, "My grace is sufficient for you." Beyond that, the Lord never explained to Paul why. It is the same with us. He offers us no exemptions and owes us no explanation. Christians get cancer. Christians go broke. Christians lose their jobs. Christians have accidents. Christians die young. Christians have birth defects. Christians have heart attacks. Christians get Parkinson's.

No promise exists that God will save us from these things, but He will strengthen us in them. He doesn't get us out. He gets us through. That is most often the way of God. He did not save Daniel from the lions' den. He saved Daniel in the lions' den. He got in the lions' den with him and shut the mouths of the lions so that they did not devour him.

He did not save the three Hebrew young men from the fiery furnace. He saved them in the fiery furnace. He got in the furnace with them and became their shield so that the fire did not consume them.

He did not route David on some outer loop around the valley of the shadow of death. David had to walk through it; but the Lord walked through it with him and brought him safely to the other side.

That's how we can endure sickness and pain. The Lord is the One who strengthens us.

Karen Kingsbury wrote in her book *Reunion*, "Human suffering is too big to get our arms around. Don't try to figure out what God's teaching you by this and don't try to understand God. If he could fit into your idea he'd be too small for any of us."[7]

Facing Death Triumphantly

Third, through Christ we can face eternity confidently. The words "I am able to do all things through Him who strengthens me" come at the conclusion of Paul's letter to the church at Philippi. When he wrote the letter, he was in prison facing the prospect of execution for preaching the gospel. He said that he stood, in a sense, at a fork in the road between life and death. He readily admitted that he really didn't know which road he would prefer to take. He was torn between the need to stay and minister for Christ and the desire to depart and be with Christ. He concluded that to depart and be with Christ was "far better." It would be a step up. It would be a promotion. It would be the best thing that could happen to him. Death for Paul would not be the lesser of two options; it would be the greater of two blessings.

Because of Christ, we need to have no real fear of death. Harley Clemons, in an interview with the late Harry Emerson Fosdick, pastor of Riverside Baptist Church in New York City, asked him if he was willing to share his view of his own death.

Dr. Fosdick replied, "I view it pretty much as I did being put to sleep recently when I had surgery. I knew little about what they would do or what the outcome would be. Yet I entered peacefully because I said to myself, 'I know my surgeon.' With a view of my own death, I trust God even more." That is our confidence also.

I read once about a lady who loved to cook and often entertained guests in her home. Her specialty was her desserts. As she prepared to clean the table she would always say to guests, "Be sure to keep your fork because the best is yet to come."

As her own death approached, she requested that they place a fork in her hand in the casket because, as she said, "the best is yet to come."

If Christ is your Savior, then it will be true of you and me also—the best is yet to come. All of us, like our friend, can survive the death of a spouse, endure a lifetime of illness, and even face death triumphantly through Christ who strengthens us.

Chapter 10

Death's Reminders

✳ Deuteronomy 34:5–9; Joshua 1:1–9 ✳

WHEN ASKED ABOUT what most surprised him in life, Billy Graham answered, "Its brevity." Too quickly for all of us, life moves to the twilight.

The shortness of life and the sureness of death bring to mind things that we need to remember about life and about death. One place where these reminders are given to us is in the account of the death of Moses. The Scriptures say that Moses died "as the LORD had said" (Deut. 34:5). After a period of mourning, the spotlight shifts from the death of Moses to the life of Joshua. He has been appointed by God and anointed by Moses as the new leader.

The Lord then commands Joshua to rise and go over the Jordan. The leadership has changed, but the mission remains the same. Israel was to press on to the Promised Land.

The text then presents a promise from the Lord to Joshua: "Haven't I commanded you: be strong and courageous? Do not be afraid or discouraged, for the LORD your God is with you wherever you go" (Josh. 1:9).

Two important truths emerge about life and death from this experience:

Our Lives Are in God's Hands

The Scriptures say simply, "Moses . . . died . . . as the LORD had said" (Deut. 34:5). Moses did not die because he was old. He did not die because he was sick. He died because God said so. Alfred Lord Tennyson said concerning his friend Percy Shelley, "The finger of God touched him and he slept." It is so with all of us.

Alternatively, William Henley in his poem "Invictus" wrote,

> *It matters not how straight the gate*
> *How charged with punishment the scroll.*
> *I am the master of my fate.*
> *I am the captain of my soul.*

I do not know as much as I once did about life and death, but I know one thing—that statement is not true. I am not the master of my fate. I am not the captain of my soul. Neither are you. We are not always in control of what happens to us; but we are in control of our responses to these events.

The apostle James says the same thing in another way. He paints for us a picture of businessmen pouring over a map of the Mediterranean world and making their plans for the future. They anticipate going first to one city and then another to make their fortunes. The problem is, they do not take God into account. So he warns,

> Come now, you who say, "Today or tomorrow we will travel to such and such a city and spend a year there and do business and make a profit." You don't even know what tomorrow will bring—what your life will be! For you are like smoke that appears for a little while, then vanishes. Instead, you should say, "If the Lord wills, we will live and do this or that." (James 4:13–15)

We should live our lives with a conscious dependence on God. We live as He wills. While we do not know what will be tomorrow, the death of someone we know always reminds us that we're still alive—perhaps for some purpose for which we ought to reexamine, always remembering that our lives are in God's hands.

Our Lives Do Not End at the Cemetery

We live on after death in two ways—through our influence and into eternity.

The Scriptures say Moses laid his hands on Joshua (Deut. 34:9). Just so, we all touch others through our influence. Carson McCullers, wrote, "How can the dead be truly dead when they still live in the souls of those who are left behind?"[8]

We also live on in eternity. When Moses last appears in the text, he has been buried in an unmarked grave on a windswept mountainside overlooking the land he will never be privileged to enter. The services were planned and attended only by God and the angels. There are no markers. No flowers. No mourning.

It would be sad if this were the final chapter in Moses' life. Now walk with me up another mountain fourteen hundred years later. It is the Mount of Transfiguration. Jesus has taken His disciples Peter, James, and John to a high mountain where He will give to them a visual demonstration and they will hear an audible voice that declares Him to be the Son of God. As He was praying, Jesus takes on the glow of heaven as His divinity shows through. Then a voice from heaven says, "This is My beloved Son. I take delight in Him. Listen to Him!" (Matt. 17:5). Then Moses and Elijah appear with Jesus. It's obvious that Moses is alive and well. He and Elijah have come with God to attest to the fact that Jesus is God's Son.

Moses' life did not end on Mount Nebo, and ours does not end at the cemetery. We live on in eternity because of what God has done for us through Christ.

Chapter 11

Hope for the Hopeless

✳ 1 Thessalonians 4:13–18 ✳

WHEN JOSEPH ADDISON lay dying, he sent for his stepson who had lived a restless, rebellious life. When Lord Warwick arrived, Addison said to him, "I have sent for you, son, that you may see the kind of peace a Christian can have even when he is dying."

There is a difference in the way Christians and non-believers face their own deaths. The difference is hope in Jesus Christ.

Paul voices this sustaining hope when he writes in 1 Thessalonians 4:13–18:

> We do not want you to be uninformed, brothers, concerning those who are asleep, so that you will not grieve with the rest, who have no hope. Since we believe that Jesus died and rose again, in the same way God will bring with Him those who have fallen asleep through Jesus. For we say this to you by a revelation from the Lord: We who are still alive at the Lord's coming will

certainly have no advantage over those who have fallen asleep. For the Lord Himself will descend from heaven with a shout, with the archangel's voice, and with the trumpet of God, and the dead in Christ will rise first. Then we who are still alive will be caught up together with them in the clouds to meet the Lord in the air and so we will always be with the Lord. Therefore encourage one another with these words.

In these verses, Paul shares with us three truths that give us hope. For a moment, ponder these with me.

A New Concept of Death

Paul describes the dead as "those who have fallen asleep . . ." (v. 14). The word *asleep* is the New Testament's favorite word for the death of a Christian; in fact, it is translated seventeen times into English. What does this word *asleep* mean?

Imagine a man coming home after a hard day's work. He sits down in his easy chair to rest and read the paper before the evening meal. After a few moments of relaxation, he dozes off to sleep. There is nothing dreadful or fearful about that. In fact, it is a welcomed and enjoyable experience. That's the word the Bible uses to describe the death of a Christian.

Catherine Marshall, in her helpful book *Beyond Ourselves*, tells of a friend whose teenage boy died of diabetes a few months before insulin was discovered. She said her son suspected he was going to die and asked his mother, "Mother, what is it like to die? Mother, does it hurt?"

"I remember," she said, "that I fled to the kitchen, supposedly to attend to something on the stove. I leaned against the kitchen cabinet. Queer, I'll never forget certain tiny details, like the feel of my knuckle pressed hard against the smooth, cold surface, as I asked God how to answer my boy.

"God did tell me. Only He could have given me the answer to the hardest question that a mother can ever be asked. I knew—just knew how to explain death to him. 'Kenneth,' I remember saying, 'you know how when you were a tiny boy, you used to play so hard all day that when night came, you would be too tired to undress—so you would tumble into Mother's bed and fall asleep? That was not your bed. It was not where you belonged. And you would only stay there a little while. In the morning to your surprise you would wake up and find yourself in your own bed in your own room. You were there because someone who loved you had taken care of you. Your father had come with his gentle strong arms and carried you away.'

"So, I told Kenneth that death is like that. We just wake up some morning and find ourselves in another room—our own room, where we belong. We shall be there because God loves us even more than our human fathers and takes care of us just as tenderly."

To his and his mother's hopeful comfort, "Kenneth never had any fear of dying after that."

What's it like to die? Does it hurt? No, not if you are a Christian. It is like going to sleep and waking up in your own room in your Father's house.

A New Certainty of Resurrection

The apostle Paul shares a second truth about hope in verse 14 when he says,

> Since we believe that Jesus died and rose again, in the same way God will bring with Him those who have fallen sleep through Jesus. (1 Thess. 4:14)

This verse expresses the certainty of the resurrection. When Paul describes what happened to Jesus, he does not say that Jesus went to sleep. He speaks specifically of *death*. That's because on the cross Jesus suffered the agony, heartache, and misery of all our sins. He died that we might know sleep.

In 1 Corinthians 15:20, the apostle Paul describes Jesus as the "firstfruits of those who have fallen asleep." The word *firstfruits* is an agricultural term. It describes those first heads of grain that get ripe in the field in late spring or early summer. These firstfruits were very special to the Jews. They were the beginning of the harvest and pledge of more to come. If there were no firstfruits, there would be no harvest later. If there was no beginning, there would be no reason to expect an end. These were so important that they were offered as a sacrifice to God.

Jesus is the firstfruits of the resurrection. He is the beginning of the resurrection, and He is God's pledge to us that there shall be a general resurrection at the end of time. So, if anyone should ask you, "When is the resurrection going to begin?" you should tell them, "It is already started. It started when Jesus was raised from the dead." And if anyone should ask you, "How can I be sure there is going to be a resurrection?" you may tell him, "You can be sure because Jesus was raised from the dead."

The blessed hope of the believer is that Jesus is going to return to the earth. When He does, the graves in the cemeteries will be opened and the dead shall be resurrected just as He was resurrected. If we are fortunate enough to be alive when He comes again, our bodies will then be transformed without having to go through the death experience. We have the great certainty of this great resurrection because of what Jesus did and said.

A New Confirmation

Finally, Paul writes in 1 Thessalonians 4:17,

Then we who are still alive will be caught up together with them in the clouds to meet the Lord in the air and so we will always be with the Lord.

Two phrases in that verse should be noted. First, the phrase "with them" means we will be with our loved ones forever. Second, we will be "with the Lord." Both speak of the glad reunion we will experience in heaven. We will be with our loved ones and we will be with the Lord forever. This gives us hope and comfort.

One of the last letters from the pen of the well-beloved and famous minister, F. B. Meyer, reads like this:

I have just been told, much to my surprise, that I have but a few days to live. It may be, by the time this reaches you, I shall have entered the palace. You need not bother to answer. I shall see you in the morning. Yours very truly, F. B. Meyer.

All of God's people can say that. It may be that before those of us here today ever meet again, some of us will have passed beyond. Never mind, we shall meet again—in the morning.

When Jesus comes again, the graves shall be opened, the dead shall be raised, and the living shall be transformed. Then we shall be together and be with Him forever. Are you ready for His coming? You can be prepared by trusting Him as Savior and joyfully submitting to Him as Lord.

Through Jesus, then, we have a new concept of death. We have the certainty of the resurrection and confirmation of a glad reunion.

He gives hope to the hopeless.

Chapter 12

A Voice from Heaven

✳ Revelation 14:13 ✳

SOMETIME AGO I received a letter from a woman in Wisconsin whose daughter had been brutally murdered eleven years earlier. Someone shared with her one of my books and she wrote to ask, "Do you know what heaven is like? Has anyone ever come back from there to tell us about it?"

Her letter and her question reveal the deep longings of our hearts today. When we come to a place like this, when we have lost a loved one, we want to know, "Does heaven have anything to say to us?"

The answer, of course, is "yes." Listen to the risen Christ as He answered her question and ours: "Then I heard a voice from heaven saying, 'Write: The dead who die in the Lord from now on are blessed.' 'Yes,' says the Spirit, 'let them rest from their labors, for their works follow them!'" (Rev. 14:13).

So what is heaven like? The risen Lord tells us it is a place of joy for the believer, rest for the weary, and reward for the faithful.

Heaven Is a Place of Joy for the Believer

The word *blessed* literally means "happy, fortunate, to be congratulated." Joy—real joy—is mentioned frequently in Scripture. Look at what God says to us about joy:

In Your presence is abundant joy. (Ps. 16:11)

This is the day the LORD has made; let us rejoice and be glad in it. (Ps. 118:24)

David, because of his sin, lost the joy of his relationship with God and so he cried out, "Restore the joy of Your salvation to me" (Ps. 51:12).

In announcing the birth of Jesus to the shepherds, the angels said, "Don't be afraid, for look, I proclaim to you good news of great joy that will for all the people: Today a Savior, who is Messiah the Lord, was born for you in the city of David" (Luke 2:10–11).

In the most joyous book in the New Testament, the apostle Paul writes, "Rejoice in the Lord always. I will say it again: Rejoice!" (Phil. 4:4).

"But," you ask, "is there some special word for me in my sorrow?" Yes, the Scriptures say, "Weeping may spend the night, but there is joy in the morning" (Ps. 30:5). For some of you, it has been a long, long night. You may feel as if you've been on the graveyard shift; but remember, morning is coming and in His presence there is fullness of joy.

Heaven Is a Place of Rest for the Weary

Rest is a beautiful word. It conjures in our minds the idea of an easy chair after a hard day's work, home after a long journey, relaxation after a stressful job.

We all need rest from time to time. For the children of Israel, traveling through the wilderness for forty years was a wearying experience. They grew weary of the burning sand of the Sinai Peninsula, the blistering sun of the eastern sky, and of constantly living in tents. They longed for the journey to end and finally to reach the Promised Land. The Lord spoke of this journeying as entering into His "rest" (Heb. 4:3). The writer of Hebrews uses this picture of resting in Jesus Christ as an anchor for the soul of the believer. When the struggles of life are over and the journey has come to an end, we will rest at last in our eternal home—heaven with Christ.

The Scottish Presbyterian reformer, John Knox, once said, "The world be weary of me and I be weary of it."[9] Life can be wearying for all of us; but rest *is* available—in Jesus Christ and in heaven; in life and in death.

Listen then to the words of Jesus to us today, "Come to Me, all of you who are weary and burdened, and I will give you rest. All of you, take up My yoke and learn from Me, because I am gentle and humble in heart, and you will find rest for yourselves. For My yoke is easy, and My burden is light" (Matt. 11:28–30).

Heaven Is a Reward for the Faithful

"The dead who die in the Lord from now on are blessed. 'Yes,' says the Spirit, 'let them rest from their labors, for their works follow them!'" (Rev. 14:13).

Forensic science tells us a person can hardly go into a room without leaving some evidence he has been there—a fingerprint, a hair from his head, a bit of fabric from his clothing—something of himself. How then could we pass through this life and not leave a trace? Our moral and spiritual footprints and fingerprints are everywhere we have been. We're all making a record here on earth, and we're accountable to God for the way we live. We can't outrun our record. We can't outlive our record. We can't erase our record. It follows us into eternity.

Our eternal salvation cannot be earned because we are saved by God's grace, not our works (Eph. 2:8–9). Although heaven is a reward we cannot earn, there are rewards in heaven that are earned on earth and enjoyed in heaven. "We must all appear before the tribunal of Christ, so that each may be repaid for what he has done in the body, whether good or worthless" (2 Cor. 5:10).

The Scriptures say, "For we brought nothing into the world, and we can take nothing out" (1 Tim. 6:7). Paul, of course, was speaking of material possessions; and that is true; but another sense exists in which we did bring something into the world and we will take something out. As Leslie Egan reminds us, we bring a good deal into the world with us—a mind with which to think, physical bodies to be used in service to God and others, and talents and character to be developed.

We also take a good deal with us when we leave—the good and evil we have done, the love we've given, kindness shown, and the ways we have used our character in our lives. The least important thing about any person is what material possessions he or she may control while he or she is here. The most important is what we take with us when we leave—a testimony, a witness, a record.

The challenge, then, from the risen Christ, is, "Be faithful until death, and I will give you the crown of life." We're not to be faithful until we're tired . . . or until we're retired . . . but until we are expired.

Scripture has answered the important question about what heaven is like: a place of joy, rest, and reward. Now, you must answer an even more important question, which is whether you have reservations there. Eternal life is a gift that Jesus paid for with His own life, and gives freely to those who are willing to turn to Him for salvation.

Chapter 13

Comfort within Chaos

✳ Job 1:21 ✳

IN A SERIES of tragic calamities, Job lost all of his children and possessions. His response was simply,

> The LORD gives, and the LORD takes away. Praise the name of Yahweh. (Job 1:21)

Job loved God and his family, yet he lost all of his children, health, and fortune in a series of tragic events. Job could not understand, much less explain, why these things happened. When his "friends" tried to explain it, they just ended up looking silly and frustrated Job instead of comforting him.

I'm not going to attempt to explain the inexplicable, nor am I asking you to comprehend the incomprehensible. My prayer is to bring you some consolation from God's Word, which is where we find Job's response.

The Lord Gives

Children are a gift from God, and your precious child was no exception (Ps. 127:3). All children are a gift from God, as are the other people He sent into our lives. We do not take life or each other for granted when we tell people how much they mean to us. If you have a special memory to share with the family, I encourage you to share it with them today in person or soon in writing.

Today we will celebrate her life as a wonderful gift, even as we mourn her death as a tragic loss.

The Lord Takes Away

You may be wondering what God's role in death is. You are not alone. God did not explain His actions to Job. Perhaps because Job was in no state of mind to absorb it. For that matter, who among us is able to understand the infinite ways of God?

How unsearchable His judgments and untraceable His ways! (Rom. 11:33)

As a minister of the gospel, I wish I had more answers to give you today. There are still painful, unsolved mysteries that will not be cleared up this side of heaven. Job did not shrug off those questions, nor was he shy about asking God about them.

One thing we do know is that our separation is temporary when Jesus Christ is our Savior. It helps us to remember that, on the cross, Jesus defeated death and the devil, thus taking away the permanent sting of death.

> Death has been swallowed up in victory. Death, where is your victory? Death, where is your sting? (1 Cor. 15:54b–55)

Although we do not have all of the answers today, we do know there is more to her story that we have not yet heard. This funeral is not the final chapter of her life story or yours. Job must have known that there was more to the story because even in the darkness of his confusion, he boldly declared . . .

Blessed Be the Name of the Lord

> The LORD gives, and the LORD takes away.
> Praise [blessed be] the name of Yahweh.

Praise/blessed comes from the Hebrew word for "kneel," which is a natural posture of worship. You may not feel like worshiping today, which is understandable. You may identify more with Job's wife, who encouraged him to "curse God and die!" (Job 2:9). Job's response to her was framed in a question, "Should we accept only good from God and not adversity?" (v. 10).

King David also knew what it was like to bury his children. He wrote these powerful words in one of his lament psalms, "I will praise the LORD at *all* times; His praise will *always* be on my lips" (Ps. 34:1, emphasis mine). Anyone can praise God during times of health and wealth. David faced many obstacles and enemies in his life, including armies, a giant, his boss, and even a couple of his own sons. Perhaps his biggest test of faith was the death of his firstborn child. When David heard the bad news, he immediately stopped weeping and started worshiping, which shocked the whole palace. Worship is where healing began for David, for Job, and it will also bring healing for you.

Worship is not the expected response, which is why the Bible says that believers do not grieve like those who have no hope (1 Thess. 4:13). Christians realize that although the sting of death is very painful, it is not permanent. The pain of separation drives us to our knees, then makes us look up like broken children who are eager to receive the comfort we need within the chaos.

I invite you to bow your knee to Jesus today. Maybe for comfort. Maybe for courage. Maybe for salvation.

Chapter 14

Victory in Death Valley

✳ Psalm 23 ✳

I DOUBT THERE is a chapter in the whole Bible that has provided comfort to more people . . . ever than Psalm 23. The Bible is still the world's most read book, and Psalm 23 is likely the most widely known and beloved chapter.

Psalm 23 is special because it is David's own testimony. The first verse is perhaps the most personal and profound.

The Lord Is Pastoring Me (v. 1)

When David says, "The LORD is my shepherd" (v. 1), he is literally saying (singing), "Yahweh is pastoring me." *Pastor* and *shepherd* are two terms that describe the same Hebrew word. David uses the present tense throughout this psalm because he is testifying to what the Lord is currently doing in his life, not just in the good old days.

I hope that you are allowing the Lord to pastor you through Death Valley today. Human pastors are a gift from

God, but they are not substitutes for the Good Shepherd who personally wants to love and lead you through this valley of death today.

The Lord Is Providing for Me (vv. 2–3)

David boldly declares, "There is nothing I lack" (v. 1), then testifies how God is meeting his physical, emotional, and spiritual needs each day.

He provides for our physical needs by leading us to *green pastures.*

Sheep won't lie down when they are hungry. They are restless until they are full.

Funeral and estate planning unfortunately happen in the middle of a fog of grief. Ask Jesus to provide for your greatest needs in the middle of the valley of the shadow of death.

He provides for our emotional needs by leading us *beside still waters.*

Sheep obviously need water, but they are fearful of strong currents because they are bad swimmers. Have you ever tried to swim while wearing a wool coat? When sheep approach a swollen stream, their survival instincts are conflicted by both a craving for water and fear of drowning. A good shepherd will create still waters by building a makeshift dam of stones, which form a calm pool from which they will drink.

Living in a constant state of anxiety will rob our souls of joy. Ask your Good Shepherd to lead you beside calm "waters of rest" today.

He provides for our spiritual needs by *restoring our souls*.

King David lost his way spiritually a few times, breaking several commandments along the way. He faltered to covetousness, adultery, murder, lying, etc. Even shepherds need a Shepherd to lead them back to spiritual health.

We all went astray like sheep. (Isa. 53:6)

Sheep can't see fifteen yards ahead of them, so, they constantly wander off and get lost. David shows us a better way:

He leads me along the right paths for His name's sake. (Ps. 23:3)

If you have wandered away from your faith, I can't think of a better time to ask the Good Shepherd to lead you back to Him. Jesus wants to restore and renew your life today.

The Lord Is Protecting Me (vv. 4–6)

"Even when I go through the darkest valley, I fear no danger [evil], for You are with me; Your rod and Your staff—they comfort me" (v. 4).

Mountains and valleys create pinch points for predators and thieves. When the sun is obstructed in valleys, dark shadows appear. Some scholars believe the dark valley David is picturing is a real place in Israel between Jericho and Jerusalem, used as the setting for Jesus' good Samaritan parable.

Our Good Shepherd leads us through dark, dangerous valleys so that we don't need to fear going through them. The two darkest valleys people fear are death and evil, neither of which intimidated David. Nor should they intimidate you today.

You don't need to fear death today.

David lost his first son shortly after his birth. Scholars believe that David wrote this psalm soon after another son, Absalom, perished in an unsuccessful coup for the throne. The death of a child is perhaps the darkest valley through which anyone can travel.

Pastors often come alongside parents as they must walk through the valley of the shadow of death, having lost their own children. One such incident involved a dear couple who lost two teenage sons in an automobile accident. Such a dark night would be unbearable apart from the fear-dispelling presence of faith in the Good Shepherd. Psalm 23 provides assurance that Christ's sheep need not walk through this dark valley either alone or in fear.

> I go *through* the darkest valley. (v. 4, emphasis added)

Vance Havner, having lost his wife of thirty-six years, said, "I am still in the valley, but thank God I am walking through it, not wallowing in it."[10]

You don't need to fear evil today.

> I fear no danger [evil], for You are with me. (v. 4)

Evil/danger (*ra'*) is a generic term in Hebrew describing bad things like moral evil and calamity. While our own death is a future dilemma, evil is a daily dilemma staring us in the face each morning. Christians do not need to be terrified of terrorism, panic over politics, or have angst over the economy.

Evil doesn't need to be feared; it needs to be conquered. "Do not be conquered by evil, but conquer evil with good" (Rom. 12:21).

> You are with me; Your rod and Your staff—they comfort me. (Ps. 23:4)

The shepherd's *rod* was a two-by-three-foot club used as a weapon.

The shepherd's *staff* was a long walking stick with a crook/hook. They used it to nudge wayward sheep or lift a newborn lamb to its mother.

While the rod protects us from our external enemies, the staff protects us from our internal enemy—ourselves. The everyday shepherd's tools in the hands of the Good Shepherd gave comfort to David, and they will comfort to you today as well.

Eventually we will all walk through the valley of the shadow of death (Heb. 9:27), but we don't have to be intimidated by death or conquered by evil.

Chapter 15

Putting Your House
in Order

✳ Genesis 23 ✳

(THIS SERMON MAY be better suited for a worship service than a funeral service, which, by the way, can be one and the same.)

We may not have much control over when we leave this planet, but we do have a say in how we leave and the impact it will have on our families. When King Hezekiah became terminally ill, the prophet Isaiah said to him,

> This is what the LORD says: "Put your affairs [house]
> in order, for you are about to die." (2 Kings 20:1)

Abraham is an even better example of how to put our houses in order because he didn't have the advance warning that Hezekiah had, and neither do we. I can think of at least four ways Abraham showed us how to put our houses in order before our funeral.

By Updating Our Financial Affairs

Very few people can relate to the size of Abraham's vast estate, but we all have something of value to leave our family members. Sentimental value is as important to some people as financial value, which can lead to family friction. This can be minimized or altogether avoided during a time of grief when a will or trust has been prepared.

"If anyone does not provide for his own, that is his own household, he has denied the faith and is worse than an unbeliever" (1 Tim. 5:8). *To provide* (*pro-video*) literally means "to see or plan ahead."

More than half (55 percent) of Americans will die without a will or trust, according to the American Bar Association. Almost half do not currently have any life insurance. There is a better way to live and a better way to leave.

Shortly after his wife, Sarah, died, Abraham not only bought a funeral plot, he bought a whole cemetery! It was technically a nice cave, which was the upscale equivalent of a cemetery in that culture. Almost forty years after Abraham bought that cave, his sons had an awkward reunion at their father's funeral. It is worth noting that neither son debated details about their inheritance because Abraham had already prearranged it all in writing (Gen. 25).

What do you need to do to put your financial affairs in order before your funeral?

By Formalizing Our Funeral Plans

It is understandable why some people don't like to talk about death, but you don't have to like death in order to get ready for it. The less decisions your family has to make when you die, the better.

Many of Abraham's family members were likely buried in that family cemetery, like his great-grandson Joseph. Does your family have a written account of what your funeral preferences and plans are? You can put your house in order by simply formalizing where or how you wish to be buried. This will comfort and bless your family in that inevitable hour of grief.

By Mending Our Family Fences

Abraham did not have a perfect family track record. For that matter, who does? He lied to, about, and with Sarah more than once. Sarah pushed him into fathering an illegitimate child because they both grew tired of waiting for the one God promised them.

Favoritism between these two sons ran rampant in Abraham's dysfunctional home and unfortunately became a family tradition. That favoritism was passed down to succeeding generations, which still impacts some global conflicts today.

Is there any unfinished family business that you have been putting off? Perhaps there is a family feud you can help settle or a person you need to forgive.

By Getting Right with God

"He took his last breath and died at a ripe old age [175], old and contented, and he was gathered to his people" (Gen. 25:8).

Even more commendable than the length of Abraham's years, were the quality of them. His early pioneering faith took him from his hometown of Ur to a far-off frontier called Canaan, where he would live for an additional one hundred years. Eventually the Promised Land and promised Son would become the legacies of this patriarch.

The greatest comfort you can give your loved ones in their time of grief is to have a clear testimony of your relationship with Jesus Christ, God's Son of promise. Christians place their hope and eternity in the finished work of Jesus on the cross. Will your faith story bring hope and clarity or confusion and sorrow at your funeral? Make sure your relationship to God is in order today, not only for your sake, but for those who love you and want to see you again in heaven.

Abraham's family benefited not only from how he lived, but how he died. So can yours.

Conclusion

After the Funeral Is Over

THE WIFE OF Duke McCall, retired president of The Southern Baptist Theological Seminary and former president of the Baptist World Alliance, died several years ago. In explaining some of his feelings, Dr. McCall wrote, "After a church service, a well-intentioned acquaintance caught me off guard by saying, 'I am sorry you lost your wife.' Before I could edit my response I said, 'I did not lose my wife. I know where Marguerite is. I am the one who is lost.'"

Anyone who has had a loved one die knows how devastating it can be. It leaves you disoriented, distraught, and lost. It takes us a long time to find ourselves.

The pastor who is really interested in "healing the brokenhearted" soon realizes that his work is not finished when he has preached the funeral sermon or conducted the graveside service. Grief goes on and so must our ministry to the grieving.

What can the minister say and do at such a time that will be helpful to the family? There is no one dramatic gesture or pearl of wisdom that will dissolve the heartache, but there are many acts of ministry that can convey your concern and help to soften the blow that the person has suffered.

I offer several practical suggestions learned from personal experience as a pastor who also wrestled with the awkwardness of what to do after the funeral as over.

Be There for Them

For a long time I dreaded going to see people when they had lost a loved one because I thought I had to say something comforting and I didn't know what to say. In time I realized, however, that words may not be the primary need of grieving people. Your presence is what counts. This is the first thing the bereaved needs above all else. Long after they have forgotten what you say they remember that you came.

Even a government agency like NASA recognizes the importance of being there. Following the fire and explosion that destroyed the *Challenger* space shuttle, the families of each of the seven astronauts who died had another astronaut family at their side soon after the disaster. The support families were there to help the *Challenger* families with everything from travel and food arrangements to boarding the family pet.

"With all the vast technology of our space age," said Clark Covington, manager of the Space-Station Project at NASA's Johnson Space Center in Houston, "there is still nothing more powerful than one human being reaching out to another."

Help Them Understand Their Grief

Grief is a person's reaction to a loss. The more meaningful the loss, the more intense the grief. Many people, when they experience grief, wonder what is happening to them. When there comes a numbness of spirit, the loss of memory, the trembling of limbs, they wonder, *Am I dying, too?* When the tears come uncontrollably—or not at all—when they can't sleep, when they have feelings of anxiety, fear, anger, and guilt, they wonder, *Am I going crazy?* or *Is there something wrong with me?*

Actually, each of these can be a normal part of the grieving process, and it is important, to help people understand that.

As in *Gulliver's Travels*, where Gulliver lay tied to the earth by the stakes and ropes of the Lilliputians, so the grief sufferer, too, is bound by a thousand emotional cords to the person who has died. These ties are not loosed easily or quickly.

A widower may come home from work at night and open the door to the aroma of his wife's cooking—though nothing is on the stove. If you ask a widow, she will tell you her husband is dead, but she may also tell you that she hears him in the kitchen at night, getting a snack as he often did in life. She is struggling with separation. Her husband is gone, but her memory is vividly present, and she misses him terribly. A widow may continue to set two plates at the dinner table for months. She reaches out to touch him in the bed.

Spouses may even find themselves talking to their dead mate long after they are gone. The husband of a friend of mine died. In their thirty-five years of marriage she had never taken out the garbage. He always did that. She was putting out the garbage one day, and before she thought she looked up and said, "See what you've done, Charlie. You left me and now I have to do something I never did before. I have to carry out the garbage."

Several years ago a teenager in our church was killed in an automobile accident. After the funeral his mother asked me, "Do you think it will be okay if I talk to Kirk?" I said, "Yes, I think so." Then I told her what the late Peter Marshall once said: "Those we love are with the Lord. The Lord has promised to be with us. Now, if they are with Him and He is with us, they can't be far away."

Be a Good Listener

For most people, talking is an effective means of releasing emotions and undergoing healing. So listen! That will help as much as anything you do.

In their grief people may ask, "Why, God?" "Why did this happen to me?" Don't be a glib Bible quoter. Simplistic answers to complex questions are not only unhelpful, they can be harmful. Statements like, "This is God's will," or "God knows best," are theologically shallow and provide little or no comfort. It is better to hear their questions as cries of pain rather than literal questions.

You needn't attempt to tell the bereaved how he or she feels. To say, for example, "You must feel relieved now that he is out of pain" is presumptuous. Even to say, "I know how you feel" is questionable unless someone has told you his feelings. I know how I feel about my father's death. I really don't know how you feel about your father's death. Learn from the mourner. Don't instruct.

Let Them Express Their Grief

Grief resembles steam in a steam engine; unless it can escape in a controlled way, pressure builds up and the boiler explodes. Grief work must be done. Grief work will be done. Sooner or later, correctly or incorrectly, completely or incompletely, in a creative or distorted manner, the work will be done. So emotional release should be encouraged. Comments like, "Be strong," or "You've got to hold up for others," tells the person it's not okay to cry, to hurt, or to be angry; it's only okay to "be strong." Holding the person's hand or putting your arm around his or her shoulder indicates that it's okay to grieve.

One way to express grief is through tears. There is a Jewish proverb that says, "What soap is to the body, tears are to the soul." Tears can help cleanse the soul.

Some people think that faith and tears don't mix. They think a sturdy faith in God and the promise of life eternal are out of keeping with sobbing and a display of grief. But grief does not deny faith.

When Mary and her companions took Jesus to the town cemetery where Lazarus was buried, Christ stood before the tomb. The text states simply and profoundly, "Jesus wept" (John 11:35). Those simple words speak volumes about the inner feelings of Jesus and His reaction to grief at the death of His friend.

Stay in Touch

One way to stay in touch is by mail. When I was a pastor I made a practice each Christmas and New Year season of writing a note to each member of my congregation who had lost a loved one during the year. Holidays are the worst times of the year for grieving people, and Christmas is the hardest of all the holidays.

In the notes I spoke of my love for the deceased and my concern for and availability to them especially at that time. It was a simple gesture, but it was one of the most appreciated things I did.

Help Them Help Others

Helping mourners do something useful for someone else will, in turn, help them. Activity is a crucial ingredient to the healing process.

Jesus is our model for ministry as well as our master. When His friend Lazarus died, He went and He wept and He witnessed—after the funeral was over. That's what we must do also if we are to help heal the brokenhearted.

Appendix A:
Preparation of the
Funeral Sermon

AT THE OUTSET of His earthly ministry, Jesus stood in the synagogue in Nazareth and read from Isaiah the prophet, "The Spirit of the Lord is on Me, because He has anointed Me to preach good news to the poor. He has sent Me to proclaim freedom to the captives and recovery of sight to the blind, to set free the oppressed, to proclaim the year of the Lord's favor" (Luke 4:18–19).

If ministers today are to be true to their calling, they must make Jesus' priorities their priorities. High on this list must be the work of "healing the brokenhearted." How do we do this? We do it, in part, through ministering to people in times of sorrow and death through the funeral sermon. This is no easy assignment for several reasons. First, it is because we must deal with people in the most traumatic time of their lives. Second, death often comes with such short notice that there is little time to prepare the funeral message in advance. With all the other demands placed upon him and such a short time to prepare, the minister may be tempted just to muddle through the sermon.

Somehow, some way, the busy pastor must find time to prepare and preach effective funeral messages. One thing that helped me was to develop a dozen good funeral messages that clearly and concisely set out the Christian view of death and our hope in Christ. Some of these were prepared and preached as regular sermons and then condensed and polished for use in funerals. By using this method I developed a variety of texts, illustrations, and outlines. Once prepared, I used these sermons again and again, choosing the appropriate text and emphasis for each occasion. Periodically I added a new sermon to the collection so that by mid-ministry I had an ample supply of well-prepared sermons for almost every circumstance. Then when a funeral came in the midst of a hectic workload, I was already prepared. My only regret is that I did not do this earlier in my ministry. I think this approach would help any minister—especially young pastors.

Here are three basic suggestions that I offer concerning the preparation of funeral sermons.

Be Biblical

The question of the ages was first posed by Job: "When a man dies, will he come back to life?" (Job 14:14). Through the years, people have sought to find an answer to that question in science, in nature, and in human reason. Ever since Raymond Moody's best-selling *Life After Life* was published in 1975, near-death experiences have fascinated many Americans. To many people, accounts of near-death experiences bolster the belief that dying is not an end, but a transition to another realm, a place so blissful and love-filled that people who have approached it are reluctant to return to the earthly world.

The only certain word, however, concerning life after death comes from God's Word. The only real assurance of life after death rests in the death, burial, and resurrection of Jesus Christ. Because He lives, we shall live also. So, root your funeral message in God's Word as it centers in Christ and you will offer real assurance and real comfort and real hope to people.

Be Personal

Death is not a factory gate through which people go in crowds. It is a turnstile through which they go one by one. Remember this when you preach the funeral sermon. It will help you make the sermon personal.

The pastor should take time to talk with the family of the deceased before the funeral and learn something about him or her. Every person is special and unique, and by visiting with the family you can learn something about the birth, work, background, character, age, or family of the deceased that will allow you to add a much appreciated personal word about him or her. A few well-chosen personal remarks can transform a cold, formal message into a warm, personal word of comfort and hope.

A word of caution, however: Don't talk too much about the deceased. Focus mostly on Jesus Christ. He is our hope and our comforter.

Be Brief

The funeral service should be characterized by orderliness, simplicity, and brevity. With music and message combined, the funeral service should not last more than thirty minutes. A well-prepared message can say all that needs to be said and can be absorbed by a grieving family in ten to fifteen minutes.

If we are to fulfill our calling as ministers, a part of which is to heal the brokenhearted, we must become masters at the craft of funeral sermons. Our ministry to the bereaved is too great to be taken lightly.

Appendix B:
Funeral for a Suicide

SUICIDE IS PERHAPS the most tragic form of death for a family to endure and the most difficult kind of funeral for a minister to conduct. Not only does a suicide leave the family of the deceased devastated by grief, but it leaves them to deal with a host of other emotions—guilt, embarrassment, anger, and fear.

One lady wrote concerning her mother's long past suicide: "I can't describe the hell she has put me through these last fourteen years. There has not been a day I haven't thought that, had I known, I could have helped her. Everyone knows how much I look and act like my mother. Even our hands are alike. I have bouts of being mad at her because she left me of her own free will. It's bad enough when a parent gets sick and dies, but what she did to me was cruel. I worry that I will do the same thing when I get to be her age. My daughter looks and acts like me. Will she do it too?"

Having been called to minister to the families of suicides on several occasions, let me offer these suggestions for such a funeral:

First, do not mention how the deceased died unless the family wishes you to. Place the emphasis on the hope we have in Christ and the strength we receive from Christ rather than upon the way the person died.

Second, avoid trying to give simple, trite answers to complex problems. We don't have to be able to explain everything that happens. Life is not a series of riddles to be explained. It is a series of experiences to be borne and lived through. The job of the minister is to help people bear up and live through this tragedy, not necessarily to understand it.

Finally, don't be judgmental. We never know the problems or pressures another person faces. We do not know how many valiant battles the deceased fought and won before he or she lost this final one. Each of us probably has a final breaking point. Life puts far more pressure on some than on others. Some people have more stamina than others.

Above all, be gentle and supportive. People will never need the comfort and hope and strength of Christ more than they do now.

Notes

1. Talmage C. Johnson, *Look for the Dawn!: Sermons of Courage, Hope, and Faith for Crucial War and Postwar Days* (Nashville, TN: Broadman, 1943), 58.

2. This sermon is adapted from Paul Powell, *Death from the Other Side: Your Ministry to the Bereaved* (Nashville, TN: SBC Annuity Board, 1991).

3. John S. D. Eisenhower, *General Ike: A Personal Reminiscence* (New York, NY: Free Press, 2004), 236.

4. Karen Kingsbury, *Reunion* (Carol Stream, IL: Tyndale House, 2004), 364.

5. Tim Funk, "Q&A: Billy Graham at 90," *Christianity Today*, Thursday, November 7, 2008.

6. Philip Yancey, *Reaching for the Invisible God: What I Can Expect from a Relationship to God* (Grand Rapids, MI: Zondervan, 2000).

7. Karen Kingsbury, *Reunion* (Carol Stream, IL: Tyndale House, 2009), 363.

8. Carson McCullers, *The Heart Is a Lonely Hunter* (New York, NY: Mariner Books, 2000), 333.

9. Craig and Janet Parshall, *The Crown of Fire* (Eugene, OR: Harvest House, 2005), 41.

10. Vance Havner, *Though the Valley* (Grand Rapids, MI: Revell, 1974).